Strategic Grace: The Woman's Guide to Power and Presence

True confidence is built on solid ground, not quicksand. Let's build roots, not routines.

Nic Blaize

Write and Release
PUBLISHING

www.writeandreleasepublishing.com

Dedication

To my greatest works in progress —
Ariana, Dylan, and Madison.

You are the living proof of my purpose, the echo of my prayers, and the reason I rise with fire in my spirit and grace in my stride.

Ariana, your compassion, strength, and light remind me daily that crowns are not worn on the head — they are carried in the way we lead with love.
Dylan, your heart and resilience are a blueprint for future kings who will lead with integrity and protect with wisdom.
Madison, your fire, joy, and courage are reminders that our voices were never meant to be silenced — but to be sharpened and shared.

I wrote these pages with you in mind.
So that when life tests you, when the world tells you to shrink, or when you forget your brilliance — you will return here.
You will remember who you are.
And you will rise again, not just for you, but for the legacy that lives in your name.

This book is not just for you.
It is *because* of you.

With all my love,
Mom

Ephesians 2:10 — For we are God's masterpiece.

PART I: The Inner Battlefield — Confronting What's Within

1. The Lost Art of Identity
Before the labels — who were you?
Action Challenge: Write your unfiltered identity statement. Strip away job titles, roles, and expectations.

2. Faith as Strategy
Faith is not your backup plan. It's your blueprint.
Action Challenge: Map 3 past moments where your faith rerouted or elevated your path.

3. Hope Is a Tactic
Optimism isn't naive. It's necessary.
Action Challenge: List what you're hopeful for and create a "Hope Plan" with real next steps.

4. When You Lose Yourself
Grief, trauma, burnout — the holy ground of becoming.
Action Challenge: Write a goodbye letter to the version of you that couldn't go any further.

5. The Mirror Test
You can't lead if you won't look.
Action Challenge: Stand in the mirror and list 10 traits you love (or are learning to love) about yourself.

PART II: Strategic Living — Planning, Pivoting, Protecting

6. Starting Over Isn't Weakness
Reinvention is the ultimate power play.
Action Challenge: Define what "starting over" would *actually* look like for you.

Action Challenge: Define your values in love, friendship, and business.

14. Feminine Power is Leverage

Being soft, still, and spiritual can still shift nations.
Action Challenge: Identify where you've been performing masculinity to be accepted. Replace it.

15. The Unseen Politics of Womanhood

We're all playing a game. Just don't play yourself.
Action Challenge: Name the rules that keep you quiet. Break one intentionally this week.

PART IV: Influence & Impact — Owning Your Presence

16. Quiet Influence

Presence doesn't require volume.
Action Challenge: Walk into one room with stillness and watch who shifts.

17. Leverage Your Light

You don't dim to blend. You shine to guide.
Action Challenge: Write your "light legacy." How do you want people to feel when they leave you?

18. Don't Fit the Box—Burn It

No label fits a limitless woman.
Action Challenge: Choose one identity box you've outgrown and take a bold step outside of it.

19. The Single Season

Singleness is not the waiting room. It's the throne room.
Action Challenge: Create a joy list and a personal date plan. Learn to court your own magic.

20. Marriage, Grace, and Mission

A real partnership multiplies you, not mutes you.

Action Challenge: Write a mission statement for your relationship — present or future.

BONUS: Strategic Groundwork

Each chapter ends with a section called **"Root Work,"** which connects with the companion **18-Month Strategic Grace Agenda Book**, including:

- Vision board planning
- Monthly "power check-ins"
- Trigger vs. Truth tracking
- Tactical to-do's that align with your bigger "why"
- Resets, reviews, and self-celebration rituals

Acknowledgments

When you are faced with uncertainty and shock, only faith can move you through.

I am deeply grateful for the unwavering faith that was instilled in me from my youth—a faith that reminded me I couldn't stay in the basement of disappointment for too long. This book was born not from bitterness, but from breakthrough. And I could not have forged forward without the strength, prayers, and presence of the people who stood with me when I couldn't stand on my own.

To my family—both by blood and by faith—thank you.

Mom, Nicola, Granny (watching from heaven), Brian, Yvonne, Henson, Candace, Quiana, Gina (you spoke this into existence nearly two years ago), and Christy. We've laughed, we've cried, and through it all, you've listened. Your love helped me keep writing even when I didn't feel like the words would come.

To my CDCU team, colleagues, and the resilient friends who were RIFed alongside me on April Fools' Day—what a punch to the gut that day was. We stood still, shocked and in tears. But in the silence, your calls, texts, and our private groups became a lifeline. The bond we've forged is unbreakable. This book is for you—and because of you.

To my editor and to Mary at Write and Release Publishing —thank you. Thank you for honoring my style, for giving me space to pause, and for always encouraging me to move forward with clarity and purpose. You helped me take my own advice and put it on paper.

Finally, God—this is my letter to You. In my darkest moments, You've never let go. You reminded me that ceilings were made to be shattered and that You were always by my side. Every page of this book is soaked in Your grace.

With gratitude,
Nic Blaize

Introduction

Read this before you turn the page.

This book wasn't written for the woman who's always had it easy.

It was written for the woman who's lost something—her job, her way, her worth—and still dares to rise.

It was written for the woman who's questioned everything she thought she knew and is now ready to lead from a place of *strategic grace.*

I didn't set out to write a book filled with lofty theories or flowery pages meant to impress; you can use social media for that. I wrote this the way I needed to receive it—clear, honest, and powerfully grounded in truth. Each chapter is intentionally shorter than most, not because the content is light, but because the work it calls you to do is deep. It gives you just enough to ignite reflection—so you can get quiet, look inward, and actually *do* the root work that healing and elevation require.

You don't need another long-winded book to decorate your shelf. You need a strategy to live by. And *Strategic Grace* is that blueprint.

Why I Wrote This Book (and Why Now)

After nearly two decades in a high-level federal career, I found myself standing in the wreckage of an unexpected job loss. I wasn't just grieving a paycheck—I was grieving an identity. It was in that silence that God whispered, *"Write it down."*

But not just the pain.
The process.
The power.
The grace.

There were days I could barely write a paragraph, but the mission wouldn't let me quit. Because I knew this wasn't just my story—it was yours too. Whether you're starting over, leveling up, or finally choosing yourself, this book was written to help you do it with intention, integrity, and grace.

Why the 18-Month Workbook Is a Must

Healing and reinvention don't happen in one sitting. That's why this book pairs with a guided **18-month Strategic Grace Agenda Workbook**—a tool to help you set real goals, track progress, and stay accountable to the woman you're becoming. It includes monthly themes, weekly planners, grace-based prompts, and root work exercises so that this book doesn't just live on your nightstand—it lives in your *daily life.*

Because transformation isn't about a moment. It's about momentum.

A Story to Carry with You

There's a woman I coached not long ago—mid-40s, divorced, laid off, and doubting everything. She told me, "I don't even recognize myself anymore." But when I asked her to describe who she was before the world told her who to be, something changed. Her eyes lit up. Her posture straightened. She said, "I was brilliant. I was bold. I was happy."

That woman now owns her own business, speaks on stages, and mentors other women going through transitions. What changed? She stopped looking for herself in other people's opinions—and started seeing herself through her own eyes.

That's what this book is about.

Re-seeing yourself. Reclaiming your identity. Rebuilding with strategy and grace.

Women Who Got Back Up

History is filled with women who faced unimaginable setbacks—and still made history:

- **Viola Davis** grew up in poverty and trauma, but rose to become an EGOT winner and bestselling author.
- **J.K. Rowling** was a single mother on welfare before she wrote *Harry Potter*—now a literary icon.
- **Oprah Winfrey** endured abuse and rejection, yet built one of the most influential media empires in the world.
- **Frida Kahlo** turned chronic illness and heartbreak into revolutionary art that changed culture.
- **Malala Yousafzai** survived a targeted attack for going to school—and became the youngest Nobel laureate.

What do all of these women have in common?
They didn't let the moment define them.
They let the mission refine them.

And now it's your turn.

Let this book be a mirror and a map.

Let it challenge you to grow deeper, lead louder, and live with *strategic grace*.

You were made for more.

With love and truth,
Nic Blaize

Foreword

*A letter to the woman who feels stuck, silenced, or small
— but was born to command with quiet strength.*

The Inner Battlefield — Confronting What's Within

Before the world named you, God knew you. Time to remember.

— The Lost Art of Identity —

Chapter 1:

The Lost Art of Identity

... Chapter 1: The Lost Art of Identity

Before the world told you who to be — who were you?

We all start with a name.

Then come the roles.
Daughter. Student. Girlfriend. Wife. Mother. Boss. Caregiver.
Provider.
We learn to wear these titles like badges of honor. But if we're honest,
sometimes they feel more like chains.

Slowly — and sometimes without noticing — we start answering to
what we *do*, not who we *are*.
And somewhere between striving to be the good girl, the right kind
of woman, and the one who "has it all together," we begin to vanish.

Not overnight.
But in layers.

A dream deferred here.
A boundary bent there.
A silent nod when you should have spoken up.
A fake smile when your spirit was breaking.

Eventually, the girl who once ran freely — wild with vision and unfiltered laughter — becomes someone else entirely.
You don't recognize her, but you still carry her inside you.

This chapter?
Is about *her.*

Not the you that's been praised for your hustle.
Not the you that's learned to apologize for her ambition, her emotions, or her shine.
The *real* you.
The one underneath the layers.
The one who didn't wait for permission before she showed up fully.

Let's go find her again.

You Can't Lead Strategically If You're Disconnected Internally

You want to lead. Influence. Build. Be.
But there's a voice inside you asking, *"Who am I, really?"*

Not the curated version.
Not the woman they see on Instagram.
Not the one who's learned to perform strength on command.

Because *strategy without self-awareness is noise.*
And *power without identity is literally just a mask.*
You can't walk in purpose when you're living in performance. The reality is, you're just going through the motions.

Reclaiming What Was Stolen

Identity isn't just who you say you are.
It's how you see yourself — and how you treat yourself accordingly.

But if your lens is cracked by trauma, distorted by expectations, or clouded by shame, then your reflection will always look blurry — even when you're doing everything "right." Even when you appear to have the perfect life. It's simply that, an appearance.

Let's be real: you didn't lose yourself because you were careless.
You lost yourself because life kept teaching you it was safer to *be who they wanted you to be* than to show up as your whole, authentic self.

Here's where those layers usually come from:

- **Family** taught you to be a "good girl" even when it meant swallowing your truth
- **School** taught you achievement equals worth
- **Religion** may have taught you submission without voice
- **Society** taught you your beauty was currency
- **Heartbreak** taught you love was conditional
- **Culture** taught you how to behave "appropriately" based on race, age, and gender and everything else in between.

If you've ever felt disoriented in your own life, it's not because you're broken.
It's because you've been buried beneath who you *had to be* to survive.

The Unlayering Begins

It's time to take some things *off*.

Take off the version of you who only exists to keep the peace.
Take off the woman who became everything for everyone but left nothing for herself.
Take off the one who learned that silence meant safety — and softness meant weakness.

The *real you* is still there.
Not fragile. Not lost. Not gone.
Just layered.

And today, we start peeling her back — with love, with clarity, and with grace.

ACTION CHALLENGE: Write Your Identity Statement

Let's get to the root.

Who are you, beneath the performance?

Finish this sentence five times:

"I am the woman who…"

And don't make it safe.
Make it honest. Make it holy. Make it *yours*.

Examples:

- I am the woman who creates peace — even in chaos.
- I am the woman who no longer apologizes for her ambition.
- I am the woman who doesn't chase love — she builds it.
- I am the woman who breaks cycles.
- I am the woman who remembers her worth, even in silence.

You'll return to these later. This becomes your root compass.

ROOT WORK: Reflection + Rebuilding

1. Mirror Moment
Stand in front of the mirror and say your identity statement aloud.
Hold your own gaze. Don't rush. Don't flinch.
Say it until it starts to sound like truth — not hope.

2. Release Ritual
Make a list of labels and roles that no longer serve you.
Examples: "Too emotional." "Not enough." "People pleaser." "The strong one."
Now tear it, burn it (safely), or throw it out.
Make a ceremony out of letting go.

3. Journal Prompt
"What part of me have I hidden to be accepted?"
Name her.
Then write a vow to bring her back — unapologetically and intentionally.

TRUTH TO HOLD ON TO:

"If you're always being who they need, you'll never become who you were created to be."

Strategic Grace Insight:

The most dangerous woman in the room is not the loudest — she's the one who knows exactly who she is and no longer seeks validation to exist.
Let's get back to *her.*

The Inner Battlefield — Confronting What's Within

Faith isn't fragile. It's your fiercest weapon.

— Faith as Strategy —

Chapter 2:

Faith as Strategy

... Chapter 2: Faith as Strategy

Faith is not your fallback plan — it's your foundation.

Most people see faith as a feeling.
An emotion.
Something reserved for Sunday mornings or whispered prayers in the dark.

But if you're a woman who leads — in business, in family, in purpose — then faith cannot be decorative.
It must be **strategic**.

Because faith is not just about believing in God.
It's about believing in the *you* He created — even when life tries to make you forget her.

Faith is vision before evidence.
Faith is movement without a map.
Faith is walking toward the thing with no backup plan, no blueprint, and no guarantee — except this unshakable knowing:
"I may not see how this works out, but I know I'm not wrong for trusting it."

This chapter is not about religion.
It's about **alignment**.
Spiritual clarity. Kingdom mindset. Quiet certainty.

It's about knowing that when you are deeply rooted in purpose, you don't just move to get somewhere — you move because staying stuck is no longer an option.

The Divine Blueprint
When you're rebuilding your life — your career, your confidence, your future — you need more than ambition.
You need *direction*.

But most women were taught to hustle before they were taught to hear. To hear means you have to stand still long enough to hear.
To push instead of pause.
To perform instead of position.

So what happens?

We build fast but not wisely.
We accept roles, jobs, and relationships that look good on paper but leave us empty in spirit.
We settle for what's available instead of waiting for what's aligned.

But when you move with faith as strategy, the entire rhythm changes.
You start to:

- Walk away from what looks good but feels wrong
- Wait with peace instead of panic
- Recognize divine delays as protection
- Stop forcing detours that look like opportunity but lead to exhaustion

Because strategy isn't just about speed.
It's about *timing*. His timing.

And faith teaches you to honor divine timing without losing your momentum.

Your Greatest Weapon: Obedience Over Optics

Faith will often require you to move in ways that look foolish to others.

- Starting a new business at 45
- Walking away from a high-paying role because it was spiritually bankrupting you
- Saying no to a partnership that checked every box — except peace
- Staying quiet in a moment where you used to shout, because discernment said, "Not now."

To the world, it might look like fear.
But it's actually *discipline*.
To say, "I know what I see, but I trust what I sense."

Because obedience isn't weakness. It's spiritual leadership.
And when obedience becomes your operating system, you start making decisions based on purpose — not pressure.

You stop performing for applause and start preparing for assignment.

You stop asking, "Does this make sense?"
And start asking, "Is this aligned?"

That's the difference between movement and momentum.
Between distraction and destiny.

Faith Is a Filter

Faith allows you to filter every opportunity, relationship, and decision through a higher lens.

It asks:

- Is this rooted in peace — or in panic?
- Is this leading me back to myself — or away from my calling?
- Is this God's best — or just what's available?

Because everything that glitters is not gold.
And everything that's available is not anointed.
Faith helps you tell the difference.

Action Challenge: Map Your Faith Wins
Before you can move forward in faith, reflect on where it's already worked.

List 3 moments in your life where faith carried you when logic could not:

1. A time you didn't see the way, but trusted the next step anyway
2. A moment you chose peace over performance
3. A decision that felt "crazy" but led to clarity, peace, or transformation

Now answer this:

What did those moments teach you about how you're designed to move?
Are you a woman who needs certainty to feel safe? Or are you learning that peace *is* your confirmation?

ROOT WORK: Reflection + Rebuilding

1. Create a Faith Vision Board
Rather than manifesting material outcomes, build a board that reflects how you want to *feel* in the next season.
Root it in faith-driven energy: alignment, joy, peace, impact, stewardship, restoration.
Let this board guide your actions — not your ego.

2. Align or Abandon
Take a close look at your current goals, projects, and relationships.
Ask: "Is this aligned with who I am becoming — or is it only attached to who I used to be?"

Circle what aligns. Cross out what doesn't.
Release what is no longer yours to carry.

3. Journal Prompt
"Where have I been forcing what I should be releasing?"
Write it down.
Name it.
Then write a prayer, intention, or declaration to let it go — and allow space for something greater.

Truth to Hold On To

"Faith isn't blind. It sees what isn't yet visible — and moves anyway."

When you begin to use faith as your strategy, everything shifts.
Sometimes people will shift out just to make room for the people that need to shift in.
You no longer move to prove.
You move with precision, with peace, and with purpose.

And that kind of movement?
That's not just brave — it's unstoppable.

The Inner Battlefield — Confronting What's Within

Hope is not for the faint-hearted.
It's for the forward-focused.

— Hope Is a Tactic —

Chapter 3:

Hope Is a Tactic

... Chapter 3: Hope Is a Tactic

Hope is not a wish. It's a weapon.

Hope gets a bad reputation.

They call it naive.
They label it weak.
They reduce it to Pinterest quotes and vague affirmations — a thing women cling to when they don't have a plan.

But here's the truth they don't teach you in boardrooms, broken homes, or church pews:

Hopeless women don't build legacies. They just survive them.

Hope is not the absence of reality.
It's the refusal to be limited by it.
It's the discipline of seeing what *could be* while standing knee-deep in what *is*.

Hope is what makes a woman keep creating when nothing around her is cheering.
Hope is what makes her invest in the vision — even when the

evidence hasn't shown up yet.
Hope isn't soft. It isn't weak.
Hope is *strategy*.

The Strategy of the Optimist

A woman who walks in strategic grace doesn't hope aimlessly.
She hopes on purpose.
Hope, for her, is a tactical choice — a trained muscle — not some cute phrase she sprinkles over suffering.

She is a woman who:
- Sees possibility in dead ends
- Makes decisions based on vision, not trauma
- Prepares for the open door before it even appears
- Sees around the wall

She doesn't just hope *because* — she hopes *even though*.

Hope tells her, "I don't know how this ends — but I trust who I'm becoming in the process."

Because that's where the transformation happens.
Not when everything works out, but when nothing has — *yet* — and she's still moving.

That's not delusion.
That's *spiritual discipline*.

Tactical Hope Looks Like:

- Saying yes to the job you feel underqualified for, because growth doesn't require comfort
- Leaving the relationship before it finishes breaking you, because peace is no longer up for negotiation

- Buying the domain name before the business exists, because faith moves before the funds show up
- Speaking life over yourself while your emotions scream fear
- Choosing joy while grief is still sitting at the edge of your bed in the morning

Hope isn't toxic positivity.
It's not pretending everything is okay.
It's standing in the ashes of your old life and saying:

"I still believe. I still build. I still belong here."

That's what makes hope strategic.
It's not a feeling — it's a decision.

Hope Is a Warrior's Mindset

The truth is, most people are afraid to hope again.

Because disappointment taught them that belief hurts.
Because trauma taught them that preparing for the worst feels safer.
Because abandonment taught them not to expect anything lasting.

But just because something didn't work before, doesn't mean you stop hoping.
It means you learn how to hope smarter.

You stop putting hope in people.
You stop placing it in outcomes.
You start anchoring it in something higher — purpose, alignment, identity, and God.

Hope, when tethered to truth, becomes unshakable.

Action Challenge: Build a Hope Plan

This week, don't just "hope for the best."
Hope on purpose.

Step 1: Name Your Current Storm
What's the situation that feels unclear, overwhelming, or impossible right now?
Write it down in a sentence or two.

Step 2: Answer With Vision
If I believed — truly believed — that this would work in my favor,
- What would I do today?
- What would I stop worrying about?
- What action would future-me be proud of?

Step 3: Take One Tactical Step
Pick *one* move from your answers and do it.
Not someday.
Today.

Because hope without movement is just wishful thinking.
But hope with action? That's transformation.

ROOT WORK: Reflection + Rebuilding

1. The 3x3 List
List 3 things you're hopeful for in each category:
- Career
- Relationships
- Self

Now, next to each one, write a practical action you'll take *this month* to nurture that hope.
Hope isn't about waiting. It's about planting.

2. Hope Journal Prompt
Answer this:

"Where have I been acting like it's already over — when in fact, it's just beginning?"

Then write a declaration that begins with:

"Even though ____, I will ____."

Examples:
- Even though I feel behind, I will move anyway.
- Even though I was betrayed, I will trust again — wisely.
- Even though I'm scared, I will speak up.

Return to this whenever fear tries to make you freeze.

3. Quiet Time Practice
Every morning for the next 7 days, start your day with this spoken truth:

"Today I choose hope. Not because it's easy — but because it's necessary."

Repeat it out loud until it feels real. Even if your voice shakes.

Truth to Hold On To

"Hope isn't soft. It's spiritual armor. And the woman who wears it wins differently."

Hope is not the backup plan.
It's the battle plan.

And every time you move from hope — instead of from fear — you put heaven on notice that you're not just surviving.
You're building.

You're becoming.
And that is strategic grace.

PART I:

The Inner Battlefield — Confronting What's Within

Sometimes, becoming her requires unbecoming everything else.

— When You Lose Yourself —

Chapter 4:

When You Lose Yourself

... Chapter 4: When You Lose Yourself

Sometimes the breakdown is the breakthrough.

There's a kind of loss that doesn't come with a funeral.
No flowers. No casseroles. No tearful tributes.
Just a slow, private unraveling.

And yet, it is one of the most profound deaths a woman can experience —
The quiet disappearance of the woman she used to be.

She fades in the background of routines.
She gets buried under expectations.
She gets watered down in relationships that demanded more of her
performance than her presence.
And one day, you wake up and realize:

You're still functioning.
You're still producing.
You're still showing up…
But *you're gone.*

The woman who used to dream big and laugh loud —
The one who dressed for herself, believed without needing
permission, and carried light even on heavy days —
She's become a memory.

You scroll through your old photos and think:
"I used to know her.
I used to *be* her."

This chapter is for the woman who doesn't quite recognize herself anymore.
Not because she's broken — but because she's been surviving so long, she forgot what living felt like.

The Slow Erosion of Self

Losing yourself rarely happens all at once.

It starts small:
- You stay quiet one too many times to keep the peace.
- You start rearranging your identity to fit someone else's comfort.
- You convince yourself your needs are "too much."
- You shrink so someone else can feel secure.

Over time, these tiny silences add up.
You begin to accept a version of life that is numbing but familiar.
You learn to perform instead of participate.
You build a life that looks good on paper, but feels like someone else's story.

You traded your essence for acceptance.
You traded your truth for tolerance.
You traded your joy for "just get through it."

And here's what no one says out loud:
Sometimes the hardest person to walk away from… is the one you became to survive.

But if you want to rise in strategic grace, you must make peace with this truth:
You were never born just to survive.

Grief Isn't Just for Death

Grief doesn't only belong at funerals.
It belongs in quiet closets and empty cars.
It belongs in journal pages and therapy rooms.
It belongs wherever women bury parts of themselves to make it through.

We grieve:
- The opportunities we turned down because we didn't believe we were worthy
- The version of ourselves we had to hide to make others comfortable
- The dreams we delayed while supporting everyone else's
- The girl who stopped dancing, laughing, or believing without shame
- The woman that was beaten albeit sometimes not physically but she was beaten into submission

But grief is not the enemy.
Grief is information.
It tells you that something sacred was lost.

And in that grief, there is *also grace*.
Because now you know.
And once you know… you get to choose differently.

Who Are You Now?

When you lose yourself, you are not without power — you are being invited back home.

This is your permission slip:
- To reintroduce yourself without apology
- To love the woman you're becoming, even if she's not fully clear yet
- To release the roles, rules, and routines that kept you safe but stagnant

You are not broken.
You are shedding.
You are not lost.
You are returning.

You are not your trauma.
You are the testimony that followed it.

This is your becoming.

Action Challenge: Write a Goodbye Letter to Your Former Self

Find a quiet space.
Sit with your truth.
Then write a letter to the version of you that you've outgrown.

Start with:

"You got me this far, but it's time for me to go."

Tell her thank you.
Tell her what you appreciate about how she got you through.
Tell her what you're letting go of — and why.
Tell her who you're becoming now.

When you're finished, burn it (safely), bury it, or fold it and place it somewhere sacred.

Because this isn't just release.
It's reverence.
And it's time.

ROOT WORK: Reflection + Rebuilding

1. Identity Audit
Answer these in your journal:
- Who was I five years ago?

- Who did I become to survive?
- Who do I want to become next?

Now circle any part of your old self you're still carrying that no longer fits.
These are not failures — they are tools you no longer need.

2. Journal Prompt
"What part of me is missing — and what would it take to bring her back?"

Let your pen flow without editing.
Let your truth rise up without judgment.
Sometimes clarity shows up in the process, not the plan.

3. Choose a Symbol of Becoming
Find or purchase something simple:
A ring, a key, a stone, a bracelet — anything meaningful.

Let it represent the woman you're stepping into.
Let it be your anchor — a reminder that even when you feel lost, you are in rebirth.

Truth to Hold On To

"You didn't lose yourself. You outgrew a version of you that wasn't allowed to live fully."

Losing yourself isn't failure.
It's often the beginning of the most powerful comeback.

The woman you're looking for?
She's not gone.

She's just waiting for you to remember.

Let this be your return.

PART I:

The Inner Battlefield — Confronting What's Within

The woman in the mirror? She's waiting for you to believe her.

— The Mirror Test —

Chapter 5:

The Mirror Test

... Chapter 5: The Mirror Test

You can't command the room if you're still hiding from the mirror.

Let's be honest.

When was the last time you looked at yourself — really looked — and didn't feel the urge to adjust something?

No tucking.
No smoothing.
No sucking in your stomach.
No tilting your face to the "better side."

Just... being with yourself.

This isn't vanity.
This is visibility.
And until you can truly see yourself — not through the eyes of shame or survival, but through the lens of wholeness — you will keep giving power to the room instead of bringing it with you.

True confidence doesn't start in the boardroom.
It starts in the bathroom mirror — with a woman brave enough to meet her own reflection and not flinch.

The Mirror Doesn't Lie — But It Does Echo

Mirrors reflect more than our appearance.

They echo back our beliefs.
They hold silent agreements we've made with a world that tried to define us.

When you stand in the mirror and think:

"Not enough."
"Too big."
"Too old."
"Too much."
"Too little."

That is not truth.
That is programming.

And it's time to break the agreement.

Somewhere along the way, you made an unconscious pact:
- With society's impossible definition of beauty
- With the first person who made you feel invisible
- With that teenage moment that rewired your self-worth
- With a media machine that sold you your insecurities as a marketing plan
- With the partner that reminded you every day why you weren't enough

But grace reminds us:

You are not a problem to be solved.
You are not a project to constantly be improved.
You are not your waistline, your age, or your highlight reel.

You are presence.
You are brilliance.
You are whole.

And the first person who needs to see that — is you.

Why the Mirror is a Leadership Tool

This may sound strange, but one of the most powerful leadership assessments is how you talk to yourself when no one is listening.

A woman who avoids her reflection is often avoiding deeper truths:
- What she's afraid to admit she wants
- What she's exhausted from carrying
- Who she's pretending to be so she doesn't lose approval

Here's the danger:
If you cannot affirm yourself, you will seek validation in all the wrong places.
- You will overperform just to feel "enough."
- You will shrink in meetings where your voice should be leading.
- You will attach your worth to output instead of presence.
- You will tie your existence to people, places, jobs and material things.

But when a woman can stand in front of her own reflection and say, "I know who I am,"
— *not perfectly, not flawlessly, but truthfully* —
she becomes immovable.

Because she is no longer trying to borrow confidence from applause.

She brought her own.

From Critique to Connection

This chapter isn't about makeup, body image, or filters.

This is about the sacred act of seeing.

To *see* yourself is to acknowledge all the versions of you that brought you here:

- The one who kept going when no one noticed
- The one who bent herself to fit into places she had outgrown
- The one who wore a smile to survive
- The one who is finally ready to return

This is not about self-obsession.
It is about self-connection.

You must learn to look at her — your reflection — and not look away.

You must stop flinching at your own power.
Stop questioning your own voice.
Stop deferring to a world that benefits from your smallness.

The mirror is not your enemy.
It is your portal.

And when you walk through it — fully seen, fully owned, fully loved —
you rise differently.

Action Challenge: Your Mirror Mantra

For the next 7 days, stand in front of the mirror — no distractions, no adjusting, no performance.

Look yourself in the eyes and say:

"I see you.
I know what you've survived.
And I still love you."

Say it slowly.
Say it until it sounds true.
Say it until the flinch turns into a smile.
Say it until your reflection starts speaking back.

Then, write your own **mirror mantra** — not one you saw online.
Make it personal.
Make it raw.

Say it every time you pass a mirror this week.

This is how you train your brain to stay — not run — when confronted with your own brilliance.

ROOT WORK: Reflection + Rebuilding

1. Self-Image Inventory
In your journal, finish the following:
  • "The first time I remember feeling not enough was…"
  • "The lie I've believed about my appearance is…"
  • "The truth I'm ready to start telling myself is…"

These questions are not to hurt you.
They are to locate you — so you can reclaim yourself.

2. Photo Healing Ritual
Find a photo of yourself as a child.
Print it. Tape it to your mirror.

Every morning, look her in the eyes and say:

"I've got you now.
I won't abandon you again."

This is the inner girl who is still alive inside you.
She needs your voice to speak love where shame used to live.

3. Create a Grace Mirror
Transform your mirror into a declaration space.

Use sticky notes, lipstick, dry-erase markers — whatever works.

But do not write compliments.

Write **truths**.

Examples:
- "My voice is needed."
- "My body is not a battleground."
- "My presence is power."
- "My softness is not weakness."
- "My reflection is not up for debate."

Every time you pass your mirror, read them aloud.

Let the mirror become a meeting place — where the woman you are becoming shows up, every single day.

Truth to Hold On To

"Confidence doesn't begin with being seen by others.
It begins with seeing yourself — and staying."

PART II:

Strategic Living – Planning, Pivoting, Protecting

*Your boundaries should speak
louder than your breakdowns.*

— Discipline Over Drama —

Chapter 6:

Starting Over Isn't Weakness

... Chapter 6: Starting Over Isn't Weakness

Reinvention is not failure. It's a power move.

There's a lie many women have unknowingly swallowed:

That starting over is shameful. That it means you failed. That it means you were wrong.

But here's the truth:

Starting over is not weakness. It's wisdom. It's clarity. It's courage in motion.

We live in a culture that glorifies consistency but mislabels reinvention as instability. If you change your mind, they'll say you're confused. If you pivot, they'll say you're flakey. If you walk away from something that no longer serves your soul, they'll ask, "What happened?"

But they won't ask what *you discovered* in the process.
They won't ask what you outgrew.
They won't ask what it cost you to stay silent in a space that no longer fit.

And that's okay.
They don't have to understand.
Because starting over was never about them.
It's about you.

The Strategy Behind the Start

Every woman will reach a crossroads in her life where she must choose between comfort and calling.

The decision to start over is not a sign that you've lost. It's a sign that you've awakened.

Awakened to the truth that:
- You deserve alignment, not just attachment
- You're allowed to evolve, even if it confuses the people around you
- You can love a season and still leave it behind. Read that again until it sinks in

What if we rebranded starting over?

What if we called it what it really is:
- Returning to yourself
- Reclaiming your voice
- Resetting your course with intention

Starting over is a sacred act of self-leadership. It means choosing the discomfort of growth over the illusion of perfection.

The Exit Is the Entry

Sometimes the most powerful thing you can do is walk away.
Not out of bitterness.
Not out of fear.
But out of reverence — for your life, your purpose, your future.

We often ask ourselves:
- "What will they think if I leave?"
- "What if I fail again?"
- "What if it doesn't work out?"

But here's a better question:
What if it does?

What if walking away becomes the walk *toward* the version of yourself you've been praying for?

The Road Isn't Straight — But It Is Sacred

You were not made for the straight line.
You were made for the climb, the curve, the twist, the fall, the rise.
You were made for detours that reveal your depth.

Life will ask you to begin again — and again.
Each time with more truth.
Each time with more grace.
Each time with more fire in your bones.

What you rebuild after a breakdown is not just stronger — it's more aligned.

This is where legacy is born.

Who You Become in the Rebuild

Starting over doesn't just give you a new direction — it gives you back your power.

In the reset, you meet:
- The woman who is no longer willing to negotiate her peace
- The woman who listens more to her spirit than the crowd
- The woman who knows her worth is not tied to her last chapter or the chapter before that

She doesn't beg for permission.
She doesn't apologize for re-entry.
She doesn't downplay her dreams so others can feel tall.

She stands in her becoming and names it holy.

Action Challenge: Define Your Reset

Ask yourself this without flinching:

If I were brave enough to start over, what would I walk away from?
What would I walk toward?

Now, create your *Reset Vision*.

Describe in vivid detail:
* Where do you live?
* What does a day in your new life look like?
* Who are you surrounded by?
* How does it feel to wake up in this space?

Be specific. Don't write a fantasy — write a blueprint.

This is your clarity map. Return to it when fear tells you to shrink.

ROOT WORK: Reflection + Rebuilding

1. Reverse Timeline Exercise
Write down a past moment when you had to start over.

Then ask:
* What did it cost me?
* What did it give me?
* Who did I become because of it?

This reminds you that you have done hard things before — and grown through them.

2. Affirmation Shift

Write this on a sticky note and place it on your mirror, phone, or journal:

"Starting over is not a step back.
It's the beginning of something sacred, something aligned, something mine."

Repeat it aloud every morning for the next 14 days.

3. 90-Day Reset Plan

Choose one area of your life where a reset is calling:
Career. Wellness. Relationships. Creativity. Spirituality.

Now create your *90-Day Reset*:
- 3 Specific Goals
- 3 Actionable Steps
- 3 Boundaries You Will Honor
- 3 Self-Celebration Rituals (for progress, not just outcomes)

Example (Career Reset):
- Goals: Launch a consulting service, update resume, apply to 5 aligned roles
- Actions: Block 2 hours/week for job search, enroll in a virtual workshop, rebrand LinkedIn
- Boundaries: No checking email after 7pm, no toxic clients, no undervaluing my time
- Celebrations: Monthly spa day, handwritten letter to self, dance breaks after wins

This plan is your evidence that starting over can be strategic — not spontaneous.

Truth to Hold On To

"You're not behind. You're just brave enough to begin again."

PART II:

Strategic Living — Planning, Pivoting, Protecting

*Not everything that burns is
meant to break you.*

— Grace Under Fire —

Chapter 7:

The Power of the Whisper

... Chapter 7: The Power of the Whisper

Softness is not silence. It's strategic restraint.

We live in a world that confuses noise with influence.
That tells women if you're not the loudest, boldest, most aggressive voice in the room, you're not powerful.
But some of the most commanding women do not shout.
They shift rooms with presence, not performance.
They lead with a voice that doesn't beg to be heard — it demands to be felt.

A whisper isn't the absence of voice.
It's a deliberate act of power.
It's the grace-filled, discerning, self-assured restraint of a woman who doesn't need to prove what she already knows.

You don't need to match the world's volume to make an impact.
You just need to match your voice to your value.

The Myth of Volume = Power

From boardrooms to family dinners to online debates, women are often told:
- Speak louder to be taken seriously
- Be assertive to be respected
- Defend every point to prove you're strong

But strategic grace knows when to engage and when to withdraw. She doesn't default to silence — she **chooses** it when silence says more.

She knows:
- Words spoken from alignment hold more weight than noise screamed from insecurity.
- Calm is not submission. It's control.
- Presence is not about performance. It's about power rooted in purpose.

The Whisper as Weapon

The whisper is not meek.
It is meticulous.

It is:
- The pause before a powerful boundary
- The grace to walk away without dramatics
- The subtle but firm "no" that needs no explanation
- The moment you let silence speak for you when chaos tries to pull you in

The whisper shifts power dynamics because it creates space.
In that space, people must lean in.
They listen differently.

They realize: you are not reacting. You are responding. With intention. With clarity. With strength.

Choosing When to Whisper — and When Not To

Let's be clear.
This is not a call for women to stay quiet.
This is a call to use your voice as a tool, not a weapon.
To know when to be thunder — and when to be mist.
To lead from conviction, not from a need for validation.
To walk into a room knowing that your value is not up for negotiation, regardless of your volume.

The Feminine Power of Restraint

Masculine power often looks like force.
Feminine power often looks like flow.
Both can be strong — but the kind of power we're reclaiming here doesn't always break the door down.

Sometimes, it turns the knob, walks in with grace, and doesn't need to raise a single decibel to shift the atmosphere.

Because grace isn't quiet because it's scared.
It's quiet because it knows exactly who it is.

Action Challenge: Practice Strategic Silence

This week, identify one situation where you tend to overcompensate:
- Defending your decisions
- Explaining your worth
- Justifying your boundaries
- Apologizing for your brilliance

Choose silence as your response — or offer one clear, calm sentence and **let it sit**.

Afterward, journal:
- How did I feel in my body when I chose restraint?
- What did the silence teach me about my control?
- Did anything shift in the conversation or power dynamic?

ROOT WORK: Reflection + Rebuilding

1. Whisper Audit:
Ask yourself:
- Who do I get the loudest around?
- Is that because I feel safe — or because I feel the need to earn my space?
- Where in my life have I confused reaction with influence?

2. Power Practice:
Every morning this week, say aloud:

"I do not have to yell to be powerful.
I do not have to shrink to be safe.
My presence is enough."

Repeat until it roots.

3. Mirror Drill:
Stand in front of the mirror and say one powerful sentence — slowly, quietly, confidently.

Examples:
- "I know who I am."
- "I no longer need approval to move."
- "I am not afraid to be underestimated."

Watch your posture. Watch your presence.
Believe the whisper more than the shout.

Truth to Hold On To:

"The whisper is for the woman who has nothing to prove and everything to protect — especially her peace."

Strategic Living – Planning, Pivoting, Protecting

Rest is not rebellion.
It's restoration.

— Soft Life, Strong Woman —

Chapter 8:

Soft Life, Strong Woman

... Chapter 8: Soft Life, Strong Woman

Peace is not privilege — it's power.

The term "soft life" has been trending, but let's be clear: this isn't about luxury handbags or curated aesthetics. It's about liberation. It's a woman's right to *opt out* of grind culture and *opt into* her God-given grace.

The soft life isn't a phase. It's a decision. A conscious choice to pursue peace over performance. Joy over judgment. Purpose over pressure. And for women who've been conditioned to associate success with suffering, this choice is nothing short of revolutionary.

You are allowed to choose ease — not because life is easy, but because you are worthy of navigating it without destroying yourself.

The War We Were Taught to Fight

For generations, women were taught that strong meant hard. That we had to be everything, for everyone, at all times.
We were applauded for burning out — as long as we looked good doing it.
We learned to:
- Take care of everyone before ourselves
- Smile through exhaustion

- Carry burdens in silence
- Dismiss our need for rest as "weakness"

But it's not sustainable. And more importantly, it's not sacred.

You cannot lead well when you are depleted.
You cannot love well when you are in survival mode.
You cannot hear God when your nervous system is in chaos.

Softness is not luxury. It's wisdom. It's stewardship. It's strategy.

Reclaiming the Soft Life

Choosing softness doesn't mean you lose your edge. It means your edge is no longer sharp enough to cut you.

A soft life is:
- Saying no before you're empty
- Embracing joy without waiting for the other shoe to drop
- Creating environments that feel like safety, not survival
- Operating from a full cup, not fumes

Softness is the quiet confidence of a woman who trusts her worth — and refuses to overperform to prove it.

Grace and Grit Can Coexist

Let's not confuse softness with fragility.
You can still:
- Negotiate contracts
- Lead a team
- Advocate boldly
- Build empires

But now, you do it without losing yourself. Without abandoning your body. Without running your soul into the ground. You do it rooted in calm — not chaos.

The soft life is not passive. It is powerful. It's a refusal to normalize burnout.

It is grace in motion. And it is deeply strategic.

Action Challenge: Audit Your Hardness

Ask yourself:
- Where have I been hardened by survival?
- What beliefs taught me that rest is lazy?
- What would it look like to give myself permission to soften?

Now choose one space in your life — work, love, parenting, friendships — and apply this question:
"If I were truly safe, how would I show up differently?"

Then take one action this week that reflects that softness.

ROOT WORK (Reflection + Rebuilding)

1. Boundary Rebuild
Soft women have clear, unshakable boundaries.
List three areas where you've been overextending yourself.
Now write one new boundary for each.
Example:

- I will no longer respond to texts after 8 PM.
- I will not say yes when my body says no.
- I will ask for help before I reach my breaking point.

2. Journal Prompt:
"If I really believed I was safe, supported, and seen — what would I stop doing immediately?"
What would you do *more* of?

3. Daily Declaration:
"Softness is not weakness.
I am allowed to rest.
I am allowed to receive.
I rise, not by force — but by favor."

Truth to Hold On To:

"The soft life isn't luxury — it's emotional liberation. And the woman who chooses it is not giving up. She's rising differently."

PART II:

Strategic Living – Planning, Pivoting, Protecting

Being soft does not make you small. It makes you strategic.

— Feminine Power is Not a Threat —

Chapter 9:

Lead Like a Woman

.. Chapter 9: Lead Like a Woman

Leadership isn't about control — it's about clarity and care.

Let's be clear: you were never meant to shrink yourself to lead.
You were never meant to lead in a way that dishonors your nature
just to earn a seat at a table that was never built with you in mind.

You weren't called to lead like a man.
You were called to lead like a woman — in the fullness of your
strength, your intuition, your grace, and your unshakeable clarity.

We've watched women who lead with empathy be labeled
"emotional."
We've seen women who use intuition be dismissed as "unfocused."
And those who dare to speak softly, yet decisively, are often
overlooked until their results speak for them.

But here's the truth they don't teach enough:
The world doesn't change when you copy what it already rewards.
It changes when you show up differently — and *still win*.

Redefining Power

Too often, leadership has been painted with one brush: masculine, authoritative, transactional.

But when you lead like a woman — unapologetically — you access tools many overlook:

- Emotional intelligence that builds trust
- Intuition that discerns what logic can't
- Communication that connects, not just commands
- Vision that sees beyond numbers into people

This is *not* soft leadership.

This is strategic grace in action.

Leading with Precision and Presence

Women who lead with grace don't:

- Lead to be liked — they lead to build
- Pretend to have all the answers — they empower others to find theirs
- Perform — they **present**, fully and powerfully

To lead like a woman is to:

- Honor your voice without raising it
- Speak vision that others can run with
- Stay rooted in clarity even when chaos knocks
- Be direct without being destructive
- Create space for others without losing your seat
- Refuse to attack other women simply because you're broken

True feminine leadership does not dilute itself to fit old systems.

It challenges the system.

It rewrites the blueprint.

Action Challenge: Write Your Leadership Credo

Write a statement that anchors your leadership truth.
Fill in the blanks below with your authentic self:

"I lead with *(e.g., empathy, boldness, clarity)* because I believe **(e.g., people matter more than numbers)**.
My presence makes rooms feel **(e.g., safe, inspired, seen)**, and my legacy will be **(e.g., impact over ego, purpose-driven leadership)**."

Revisit this credo weekly. Let it guide your decisions, especially in moments of doubt.

ROOT WORK (Reflection + Rebuilding)

1. Audit Your Leadership Energy
- Where are you mimicking masculine leadership styles to be taken seriously?
- Are you defaulting to hustle, dominance, or rigidity?
- What aspects of your natural feminine strengths are you suppressing?

2. Reclaim Your Style
Journal your answers to:
- "What does *feminine leadership* look like for me?"
- "What rooms have I altered myself in, and what did it cost me?"

Now write this declaration:

"I no longer borrow a leadership voice that isn't mine."

3. Reset Your Model
Think of a female leader (famous or personal) who leads with strategic grace.
What qualities inspire you?

List them.

Now: how can you embody one of those qualities more intentionally this week?

Truth to Hold On To:

"Leading like a woman doesn't mean you lead smaller — it means you lead smarter."

Leadership that is rooted in grace, vision, and alignment isn't loud — it's lasting.

And you, powerful woman, weren't made to lead like them.

You were made to lead like *you*.

Strategic Living – Planning, Pivoting, Protecting

Anger isn't ugly — unprocessed anger is.

— What to Do with Your Anger —

Chapter 10:

Dream Snatcher, Not Dream Chaser

... Chapter 10: Dream Snatcher, Not Dream Chaser

Chasers beg. Snatchers build.

We've glamorized the grind.
We've been told to hustle harder, stay hungry, "never not working."
We've been taught that to chase something is noble — that if we run fast enough, long enough, eventually we'll be rewarded. Eventually we will catch it.
But what if chasing is actually a trap?

The truth is, you don't need to chase what is already yours.
You don't need to pursue your purpose like a stranger in a crowd — out of breath and out of alignment.
In Strategic Grace, we snatch.
We don't steal.
We claim.
We prepare.
We posture ourselves for what we've already been equipped to carry.

Snatching is the posture of a woman who no longer waits for permission.
She builds. She readies. She walks boldly toward what is hers — because she's done auditioning for a life she was born to lead.

The Problem with Chasing

Let's be clear: chasing is exhausting.

Chasing looks like:
- Hustling for validation instead of leading with value
- Comparing yourself to people with completely different assignments
- Moving out of anxiety, urgency, and fear of being "left behind"
- Performing instead of preparing
- Accepting crumbs and calling it favor

And it feels like:
- Burnout masked as ambition
- Scarcity disguised as strategy
- Rejection internalized as unworthiness

The more you chase, the more you subconsciously affirm that what you desire is always outside of your reach.
But when you move like a builder, not a beggar — you start making room instead of making noise.

The Power of the Snatcher

A Dream Snatcher operates with a completely different frequency.

She knows the assignment.
She trusts her pace.
She sharpens her skills, builds her network, and aligns her environment to match what she is expecting.

Snatching looks like:
- Praying with your shoes on — ready to walk through the door when it opens
- Applying for the grant, pitching the idea, or enrolling in the course without waiting to feel "ready"

- Taking up space without apology — and without overexplaining
- Letting your preparation speak louder than your panic
- Declaring what you're claiming, not just manifesting it in silence
- Knowing it will be because it was already written

You're not being aggressive.
You're being aligned.
You're not being arrogant.
You're being available — to purpose, to favor, to fulfillment.

Dream Identity Shift

At some point, chasing becomes a performance.
But building? That's the work of women who understand timing and territory.

This chapter is your reminder:
You do not need to prove your worth by being everywhere all the time.
You do not need to wait for someone to say, "You're next."
You get to say, "I'm now."

You're not behind.
You're being positioned.

And the woman who's prepared?
She won't have to beg for the blessing.
It will recognize her because she looks like what she prayed for.

Action Challenge: Identify Your Dream

Ask yourself:
"What dream have I been chasing that I now need to ALIGN with instead?"

Now go deeper:
- What would alignment look like in your daily habits?
- How would you show up if you believed the dream was already yours?
- What is one thing you've delayed because you didn't "feel ready"?

Then answer these three:
1. One thing you can do this week to prepare for it:
2. One way you've been self-sabotaging:
3. One intentional way you'll move with strategy going forward:

This is how you shift from frantic to focused.

ROOT WORK (Reflection + Rebuilding)

1. From Hustle to Harvest Audit:
Pick one area of your life — business, relationship, health, creativity — and ask:
- Is this being pursued from fear or purpose?
- If I believed it would happen in divine timing, how would I behave differently?

2. Journal Prompt:
"What am I still chasing that I already have the tools, gifts, and favor to build?"

Reflect honestly. Then list the tools you already possess.

3. Daily Declaration:
"I do not chase what is mine.
I align.
I prepare.
I receive."

Write it down. Post it up. Say it out loud every morning this week.

Truth to Hold On To:

"The woman who builds knows she doesn't have to run after anything — it will find her ready."

PART III:

Relationship Warfare — Who You Keep, What You Allow

Shrink for no one. You were born to take up space.

— Stop Shrinking —

Chapter 11:

Emotional Vampires & Energy Leaks

... Chapter 11: Emotional Vampires & Energy Leaks

Protect your peace like it pays your bills — because it does.

Let's be clear: peace is not a perk. It's not something you "earn" after doing enough.
Peace is a priority.
Peace is a practice.
Peace is a prerequisite for purpose.

And the biggest threat to your peace isn't your schedule — it's your circle.

There are people in your life who don't mean to harm you, but they drain you all the same. Not because they're evil. But because they haven't learned to feed themselves — and you've made yourself their emotional buffet.

You cannot grow while constantly shrinking for others.

You cannot lead while endlessly leaking.

You cannot create from a place of depletion.

It's time to seal the leaks. It's time to protect your emotional currency.

The Real Cost of Energy Leaks

We often overlook how much energy we're hemorrhaging trying to:
- Manage other people's moods
- Over-explain our boundaries
- Be liked instead of being well
- Fix things that aren't our responsibility

Energy leaks are subtle.
They show up in the daily sighs. The forced yeses. The resentment masked as "support."

And if you don't identify and seal those leaks, you will find yourself exhausted in the presence of people who were never supposed to have that much access in the first place.

Who Are the Emotional Vampires?

They're not all obvious. In fact, the most dangerous ones come wrapped in charm and shared history.

Some signs include:
- You feel *on edge* or *drained* after being with them
- They always center their needs but minimize yours
- You feel guilty for setting a boundary
- They create chaos and expect you to clean it up
- Their love feels conditional — based on your availability and compliance

Sometimes, they're not people at all — they're patterns:

- Overcommitment
- People-pleasing
- Overfunctioning in relationships
  These are energetic vampires too — habits that rob you of peace.

The Shift: Boundaries Over Burnout

You were not put here to be a life raft for people who won't learn to swim.

Your capacity is powerful. But it's not infinite.

Protecting your energy is not rude. It's required.

There is nothing holy or heroic about self-abandonment.

Action Challenge: Energy Inventory

Make a list of the **five people** you spend the most time communicating with — in person, on the phone, or through messages.
Next to each name, write:

- **Fills Me**
- **Drains Me**
- **Neutral**

Then ask:
- What boundary have I been afraid to enforce?
- Who needs **less access**, not more explanations?
- What is one shift I can make this week to reclaim my emotional real estate?

Start small. But start.

ROOT WORK (Reflection + Rebuilding)

1. Energy Map Exercise
In your journal, make three columns:
- Boundaries I've Broken
- Boundaries I Need
- Boundaries I Will Implement

Choose one boundary to enforce this week — no explanation, no guilt.

2. Journal Prompt
"Why do I feel guilty for protecting my energy? What am I afraid will happen?"

Let yourself be honest. Then write a truth that's stronger than the fear.

3. Emotional Closure Letter
Write a letter to someone (you don't have to send it) who's been draining you.
Say what you couldn't say.
Honor what you've learned.
Release what no longer serves you.

Then declare closure — with or without their understanding.

Truth to Hold On To:

"You are not too much — they are just too used to your self-abandonment."
Your peace is not a luxury.
Your energy is not a community pool.
You get to choose who has access to your light — and for how long.

Relationship Warfare — Who You Keep, What You Allow

A real leader goes first — even when it's scary.

— The Leader Within —

Chapter 12:

The Breadcrumber Partner

... Chapter 12: The Breadcrumber Partner

Crumbs aren't chemistry — and love isn't confusion.

There's a specific kind of heartbreak that doesn't come from being rejected. It comes from being strung along. Teased with the possibility of love but never fully chosen. It's the silent grief of *almost* — almost valued, almost prioritized, almost loved.

Breadcrumbers are skilled at keeping you on the hook with just enough to stir hope, but never enough to offer certainty. They text when they miss your attention, not your presence. They make vague promises, play the "let's just see where this goes" game, and never quite commit — but never quite let go either.

And because the world has taught women to be patient, forgiving, understanding — you stay. Hoping that crumbs might one day become a full meal.

But crumbs aren't chemistry. And confusion is not a love language.

The Breadcrumber Pattern

A breadcrumber doesn't reject you. Rejection would require clarity — and clarity would give you closure. Instead, they linger. They give you:

- A late-night "thinking of you" text, but no follow-up.
- A flirty comment on your story, but no plans to see you.
- Talk of the future, but no present investment.
- Hot-and-cold behavior that leaves you questioning your worth.

They don't want a relationship. They want reassurance.
They don't want to love you. They want to know you're still available.

Why You Stay

You don't stay because you're weak — you stay because the pattern has been normalized. You've been conditioned to believe:

- Attention equals intention.
- Potential equals commitment.
- Consistency is something you *earn,* not something you *deserve.*

And maybe, deep down, you believe this is all you're allowed to ask for — that having *something* is better than nothing. But breadcrumbs keep you emotionally malnourished. And you deserve the whole loaf.

The Emotional Toll

Breadcrumber relationships are dangerous not because of what they do — but because of what they undo. They erode your trust in yourself. You stop listening to your intuition. You start second-guessing your standards. You shrink your voice just to hold someone else's attention.

But your heart is not a consolation prize. And your time is not disposable.

Action Challenge: Break the Cycle

Make two lists:
1. **"What I'm No Longer Available For"**
   List every red flag, every behavior, every moment of settling you've experienced and accepted in the past. Call it out. Name it. Release it.
2. **"What I Now Require in Love"**
   These are not preferences. These are your standards. Your non-negotiables. Write them with authority — not apology.

ROOT WORK (Reflection + Rebuilding)

1. Love Pattern Audit:
Take inventory of your last three relationships or situationships. Ask:
- Where did I override my instincts?
- What breadcrumbs did I mistake for effort?
- How did I breadcrumb myself by accepting less than I deserve?

2. Journal Prompt:
"What made me believe I had to earn someone's consistent love?" Explore the origin of that belief — was it from childhood? A past relationship? Then, write a new truth. A new vow to yourself.

3. Declaration:
"I don't chase crumbs. I sit at the table where full love is served — or I eat alone in peace."

Truth to Hold On To:

"If it costs you clarity, self-worth, or consistency — it's too expensive."

PART III:

Relationship Warfare — Who You Keep, What You Allow

You don't have to go viral to be valuable.

— Influence is Intentional —

Chapter 13:

Evenly Yoked ≠ Carbon Copy

... Chapter 13: Evenly Yoked ≠ Carbon Copy

Alignment is not sameness. It's shared direction.

We've been sold a one-dimensional idea of compatibility — that you must be perfectly alike in order to work well together. That to be "evenly yoked" means having identical preferences, personalities, and perspectives.

But the truth is:
Sameness does not equal stability.
Compatibility is not cloning.
And love is not copy-paste.

Being evenly yoked is about movement. It's about direction, pace, purpose, and posture. It's not about having the same playlist or ordering the same coffee. It's about holding a shared **why** even if your **how** looks different.

It's about one key thing: **alignment**.
Alignment of values. Alignment of growth. Alignment of future vision.

What Evenly Yoked Really Means

Being evenly yoked isn't about walking in sync with someone who mirrors you. It's about walking beside someone who complements you — spiritually, emotionally, and directionally.

It means:
- You don't just have chemistry — you have shared purpose.
- You don't just get along — you're moving in the same direction.
- You don't compete — you complete a greater calling together.
- You don't shrink yourself to be understood — you grow because you are supported.

Evenly yoked means being equally invested in the journey, equally committed to the path, and equally willing to do the inner work that sustains love — not just sparks it.

Unequally Yoked Looks Like This:

- One person is always compromising, the other is always coasting.
- One is healing, the other is avoiding.
- One is planning the future, the other is dodging conversations.
- One grows spiritually, the other resents the light.

Unequally yoked doesn't always look dramatic. Sometimes, it's just subtle misalignment that builds into disconnect over time.

And if you're constantly dragging, explaining, or dimming — you're not partnered, you're pulling weight.

💡 Action Challenge: Define Your Relationship Values

Ask yourself:
"What do I value in a relationship beyond surface-level traits?"
Go deeper than "funny" or "cute." Consider traits that shape a life.

Write down **5 values** that anchor your relationships:
- Faith
- Honesty
- Growth
- Humor
- Stability

Then ask:
"Does the person I'm choosing reflect or reject these?"
This isn't judgment — it's clarity.

When you know what you value, you stop settling for someone who doesn't carry it.

✸ ROOT WORK (Reflection + Rebuilding)

1. Yoked Inventory
In your journal, answer:
- Where did I lower or mute my values to keep someone close?
- Have I ever confused shared trauma for shared vision?
- Where have I confused alignment with attachment?

Let yourself be honest. You cannot build truth on denial.

2. Journal Prompt
"If I stopped looking for someone who matched me perfectly, and instead sought someone who walked with me purposefully — what would change?"

Explore how your definition of partnership shifts when you focus on growth over likeness.

3. Declare This Daily
"I am not asking for perfection. I am asking for alignment — and I will not compromise it."

Your love life should be a collaboration, not a correctional project. You don't need someone who thinks like you. You need someone who respects how you think — and builds forward with you.

✍ Truth to Hold On To:

"Evenly yoked isn't about matching shoes — it's about walking the same road in sync."

PART III:

Relationship Warfare — Who You Keep, What You Allow

Your win isn't a threat to mine.
Let's build the table.

— Room for You and Them —

Chapter 14:

Feminine Power is Leverage

... Chapter 14: Feminine Power Is Leverage

Stop performing strength. Start embodying it.

You don't have to "act like a man" to be powerful.
You don't have to erase your softness to be taken seriously.
You don't have to choose between intuition and intellect, between flow and focus.

Feminine power is not less than masculine power — it's different.
And that difference is leverage.

In a world that often rewards dominance, volume, and hustle, feminine power operates in another frequency — one that is grounded in awareness, embodied wisdom, and emotional clarity. It doesn't demand the spotlight. It shifts the atmosphere without announcing itself.

This isn't about gender roles.
This is about energetic alignment — about reclaiming the power you've been taught to suppress in favor of what felt "safer" or "more acceptable."

Because true feminine power doesn't imitate.
It initiates.

It influences.
It transforms.

The Real Definition of Feminine Power

Feminine power is not:
- Passive
- Weak
- Indecisive

It is:
- Receptive, but not complacent
- Intuitive, yet strategic
- Expressive, without apology
- Vulnerable, but never without discernment

Feminine power is felt, not forced.
It doesn't need to dominate — because it understands how to draw, how to hold, how to lead without control.

And for centuries, women have been told that this is the lesser way. That the only way to lead is to replicate masculine behaviors: louder voices, rigid posture, constant productivity.

But that's not power. That's performance.
And performance is exhausting.

Why We Dim Our Feminine Energy

Let's be honest:
Many women have dulled their feminine energy to survive in rooms built for men.

They became hyper-independent, emotionally numb, and task-oriented to be taken seriously.

They stifled softness to avoid being dismissed.
They hid their nurturing nature to be labeled "a boss" instead of "too much."

But here's what we often forget:
Your intuition is data.
Your compassion is leadership.
Your empathy is innovation.
Your presence is power.

Reclaiming your feminine energy is not about rejecting masculine energy — it's about integrating both, and finally letting your feminine side take the lead in the spaces it was made for.

Leading From the Feminine

Leading from your feminine energy looks like:
- Creating connection before commanding control
- Listening fully before making decisions
- Moving with grace and trust instead of grind and panic
- Prioritizing emotional wellness without sacrificing results
- Understanding that slowing down is sometimes the fastest way to align

Feminine leadership is magnetic.
It draws results, trust, and opportunity by simply being in alignment.

Action Challenge: Feminine Power Check-In

Ask yourself:
"Where am I over-performing in masculine energy to feel safe or seen?"

Be honest. Common signs include:
- Over-scheduling and calling it "hustle"

- Withholding emotion in professional spaces to be perceived as "strong"
- Minimizing your needs in a relationship to avoid being "too much"

Now, choose one area where you will stop performing and start showing up in presence.

Be intentional. Be kind to yourself. Be consistent.

ROOT WORK

1. Reclaim the Feminine List
Answer these in your journal:
- What feminine traits do I naturally possess that I have been taught to suppress?
- When did I start associating those traits with weakness?
- What would it look like to lead with those traits now?

2. Journal Prompt
"When was the last time I felt most connected to my feminine power — not the image I present, but the truth I embody?"

Describe the moment in detail. How did you move? How did others respond? What changed in you?

Return to that version of yourself. She's still in you.

3. Declare This Daily
"I no longer mirror masculine energy to feel valid.

My feminine energy is potent, magnetic, and more than enough."

Truth to Hold On To

Feminine power doesn't shout.
It doesn't demand the center.
It doesn't need a fight to feel strong.

It moves in stillness.
It leads with wisdom.
And it shifts everything — just by being.

You are the atmosphere.
Not because you perform strength,
But because you embody it.

Relationship Warfare — Who You Keep, What You Allow

Adjust it quietly or secure it publicly. Either way, it stays on.

— Don't Touch My Crown —

Chapter 15:

The Unseen Politics of Womanhood

... Chapter 15: The Unseen Politics of Womanhood

There's a game we're playing — even when we don't know it.

Before you ever entered a boardroom, a classroom, or a relationship, you were already learning how to navigate the quiet negotiations of womanhood.

Not the politics of parties or power struggles on TV —
but the politics that play out every day in whispered expectations and unspoken penalties.

- Be pleasant, not passionate.
- Be driven, but not "too ambitious."
- Be confident, but not "too loud."
- Be nurturing, but never need too much.

This isn't paranoia. It's policy.
An invisible rulebook passed down through side-eyes, microaggressions, underpaid salaries, and unspoken consequences.

You've learned how to smile while being silenced.
You've learned how to over-perform just to be seen as average.
You've learned how to second-guess your instinct because it made someone else uncomfortable.

And the hardest part?
You were never officially taught these lessons.
You just *absorbed* them — from culture, from correction, from survival.

But awareness? That's the beginning of strategy.

The Silent Curriculum of Womanhood

No one handed you a syllabus. But you studied the rules anyway:
- Don't interrupt — even if your idea is better.
- Don't cry — even when you're breaking.
- Don't outshine — even when you're brilliant.
- Don't disagree — even when it's demeaning.

You learned how to code-switch.
How to smile when it wasn't funny.
How to downplay your gifts to keep the peace.
How to say *"It's fine"* when it wasn't — and no one asked.

But what if you could stop campaigning for value in rooms where you already *know* your worth?

What if you stopped internalizing their discomfort as your flaw?

Because the truth is:
Many women spend a lifetime being gaslit by systems designed to contain them.

And breaking free from those systems isn't rebellion.
It's remembrance — of who you were before the world edited you.

The Cost of Making Others Comfortable

Every time you shrink to fit someone's expectation,
you disconnect from your highest self.

And while playing small might keep the peace,
it also keeps you from your purpose.

Let's be honest:
Many of the rooms you walk into know exactly how valuable
you are.
They just don't want to acknowledge it —
because if they do, they'll have to compensate you, elevate you, or
compete with you.

So they minimize. They delay. They distract.
They hope you'll second-guess your gut.
They hope you'll *settle* before you realize just how powerful you are.

But this chapter is not about blame.
It's about awakening.
Because once you see the game, you can stop being played by it.

Action Challenge: Break the Silent Rule

This week, choose one rule you were taught — or absorbed — and
intentionally break it.

Examples:
- If you were taught not to take credit, *own your success out loud.*
- If you were told to keep your voice down, *speak with authority.*
- If you were made to believe "good girls don't ask for more," *negotiate boldly.*

Write the rule down. Cross it out. Then rewrite it in your own words
— and live by that instead.

ROOT WORK

1. Rewrite the Rulebook
List the unspoken rules you've followed — not because they served you, but because they protected you.
Now, one by one, rewrite them.

Original: "Don't be too assertive."
New Rule: "My clarity is not a threat. It's a gift."

Original: "Be agreeable to keep the peace."
New Rule: "Peace that costs me my voice is not peace. It's self-abandonment."

2. Journal Prompt
"What quiet message have I been living under?
And who benefits from my silence, hesitation, or self-censorship?"

Sit with that.
Then ask: "What would it cost me to stay silent another year?"

3. Daily Declaration
"I no longer play games that require me to shrink.
I will not pay the emotional toll of making others comfortable while I disappear."

Truth to Hold On To

The politics of womanhood are not imagined.
They are systemic, cultural, and often generational.

But so is your power.
So is your discernment.
So is your ability to rise —
not with bitterness,
but with *strategy and grace.*

You don't have to win every battle.

But you *do* have to stop campaigning for a seat at the table when you were born to build your own.

You are not too much.

You are not too ambitious.

You are not too loud.

You are simply no longer willing to play a game designed to keep you small.

And that? That is the beginning of your most powerful chapter yet.

PART IV:

Influence & Impact — Owning Your Presence

Success isn't a title. It's alignment.

— Redefining Success —

Chapter 16:

Quiet Influence

... Chapter 16: Quiet Influence

Some women walk in and the room shifts — and they didn't say a word.

They don't need an entrance.
They don't need a spotlight.
They don't even need to speak.

Because their presence is the punctuation.

That's the woman whose energy does what volume never could:
it *moves people.*

In a world obsessed with "visibility,"
she knows that being *rooted* is more powerful than being *recognized.*

She isn't invisible — she's intentional.
She doesn't need applause — she has alignment.
And when she shows up, everything changes — not because she's
loud, but because she's *clear.*

That is *quiet influence.*
And the woman who holds it doesn't chase attention — she
commands respect.

Influence Isn't Volume. It's Vibration.

The world often measures influence by:
- How many people follow you
- How loudly you speak
- How often you show up
- How much you post, promote, perform
- And yes, how meanspirited you are because in your mind, "you keep it real"

But real power? It doesn't need performance.
Real power lives in your *presence*.
And your presence — when it is anchored, authentic, and unapologetic — doesn't require noise to be felt.

Quiet influence says:
- "I do not need to convince you. I embody the truth."
- "I'm not here to dominate. I'm here to shift."
- "I'm not loud because I need approval. I'm intentional because I carry clarity."

The Myth of Visibility

There's a modern myth that if you're not seen constantly, you'll be forgotten.
That if you're not *loud*, you're irrelevant.
But you are not building for virality — you are building for *impact*.

The woman of quiet influence:
- Listens more than she speaks
- Discerns more than she reacts
- Moves with wisdom, not worry
- Values purpose over performance

She understands that visibility is a tool — not the goal.
Her goal is transformation. And that doesn't require a microphone.

Action Challenge: Cultivate Your Quiet Power

This week, choose one space — a meeting, a dinner, a social gathering — and enter with *intention,* not performance.

Don't over-explain.
Don't smile to soothe the room.
Don't dilute your truth.

Just show up — grounded, observant, present.

Afterward, reflect:
- What shifted in me?
- What shifted in the energy around me?
- Did I feel more or less powerful by simply *being* rather than *doing*?

Document what you discover.

ROOT WORK

1. Presence Inventory
In your journal, answer:
- Where do I feel most grounded?
- What people, environments, or activities amplify my clarity?
- What spaces or people make me feel like I have to perform?
- How can I build more of the former — and distance from the latter?

Presence is your compass. Follow it.

2. Journal Prompt
"When was the last time I felt seen — without having to say a word?"

Who were you in that moment?
How did it feel to be honored just by your presence?
Now ask yourself: "What keeps me from bringing *her* into every room?"

3. Declare This Daily
"I do not have to raise my voice to raise my vibration.
My spirit speaks louder than my words.
And I am safe in my stillness."

Truth to Hold On To

The quietest women often carry the loudest presence.
Because her energy is rooted.
Her voice is steady — even when silent.
Her power doesn't perform — it *permeates*.

She doesn't strive to be the loudest voice in the room.
She simply becomes the one no one can ignore.

Not because she fought for the spotlight —
but because she *owned* the atmosphere.

And that kind of power?
It can't be manufactured.
It's cultivated in stillness.
Refined in silence.
And wielded in *grace*.

Influence & Impact — Owning Your Presence

Elevation requires separation.
Release with love.

— Not Everyone Can Go —

Chapter 17:

Leverage Your Light

... Chapter 17: Leverage Your Light

Stop dimming what was never meant to be hidden.

Your light is not a phase.
It's not something to be tested, adjusted, or turned down to suit the mood of the room.
It is *you*.
Your essence. Your impact. Your divine design in motion.

But somewhere along the way, you were taught to make it quieter.
To make yourself smaller.
To be palatable instead of powerful.
To fit in instead of stand out.

You learned to wrap brilliance in humility so no one felt threatened.
To hide your wisdom behind "just suggestions."
To silence your shine so someone else wouldn't feel inadequate.

But here's the truth:
Dimming doesn't protect anyone.
It only deprives the world of what it desperately needs — your presence in full power.

You Were Never Meant to Blend In

The world doesn't need more carbon copies.
It needs women who *remember who they are* — and walk in it without flinching.

You don't owe anyone an apology for your:
- Vision that sees beyond limitations
- Voice that speaks with clarity
- Confidence that doesn't need permission
- Excellence that wasn't built overnight

You may have been taught that shining makes you selfish.
That standing out is arrogant.
That confidence is a threat.

But you are not here to tone yourself down to avoid discomfort.
You are here to *light the way*.

And sometimes, your light will expose shadows — not because you're trying to, but because truth reveals what pretense hides.

The Real Cost of Playing Small

Every time you dim your light:
- You minimize your influence
- You delay your divine timing
- You lower the frequency of rooms meant to rise when you enter
- You silently agree with the lie that your power is "too much"

But your radiance was *never* the problem.
Other people's discomfort with your light? That's theirs to process — not yours to internalize.

Action Challenge: Light Legacy Letter

Write a letter to yourself from the perspective of someone your presence transformed.
Not your achievements. Not your title. Just *you*.

Start with:
- "You made me feel…"
- "Your light reminded me…"
- "You helped me believe…"
- "Being around you changed how I see…"

Then pause.

Ask:
"What part of myself am I still hiding that the world needs to witness?"
That is the part you must stop denying.
That is the part someone else is praying for.

ROOT WORK

1. Glow Inventory
In your journal, list:
- *Who or what dims my light?*
- *Where do I feel the need to shrink or self-edit?*
- *What spaces allow me to be fully seen and celebrated?*

Now adjust your exposure — not your glow.
More of what fuels you.
Less of what drains you.

2. Journal Prompt
"Where did I first learn that being fully seen was unsafe or 'too much'?"

Was it a comment? A relationship? A rejection?

Identify it. Name it. Then break up with it.

Write a vow to reclaim the parts of you you've tucked away out of fear or habit.

3. Declare This Daily
"My light is not arrogance.
It is the reflection of divine creation.
I do not dim to fit in — I rise to remind others they can too."

Truth to Hold On To

"The room doesn't need your apology.
It needs your authenticity.
And your glow? It doesn't compete. It *confirms*.
It confirms that power can be radiant.
That grace can be bold.
That presence — when aligned with purpose — can light the way for generations."

PART IV:

Influence & Impact — Owning Your Presence

God's timing doesn't need your calendar.

— It's Not Too Late —

Chapter 18:

Don't Fit the Box—Burn It

... Chapter 18: Don't Fit the Box — Burn It

You were not created to be digestible. You were created to be undeniable.

The world doesn't know what to do with a woman who refuses to be contained.

It prefers boxes. Labels. Categories that are easy to control, predict, and package.
Women who don't rock the boat. Who stay polite. Who keep their brilliance at a manageable level.
Women who check all the boxes but forget their worth in the process.

You were never called to be palatable.
You were called to be powerful.
To be too much for small minds and just enough for your God-given mission.

So when they hand you a box — smile, thank them for their concern, and burn it to the ground.

What Boxed Living Costs You

They may praise your compliance.
They may reward your ability to "stay in line."
But what they don't tell you is that every time you contort yourself to fit in, you abandon a piece of your voice, your identity, your power.

Here's what boxed living often creates:
- Quiet resentment masked as gratitude
- Repressed creativity hidden under "responsibility"
- A performative life that checks all the boxes — but feeds none of your soul

The woman who *seems* to have it all but wakes up feeling like nothing?

She's likely living in a box someone else built.

Why We Stay Boxed

Boxes feel safe.
They offer:
- Predictable approval
- A pre-written identity
- Clear rules on how to earn love or acceptance

But they also demand:
- Silence in the face of injustice
- Sacrifice of authenticity
- Self-abandonment for comfort

Boxes are cozy prisons.
And every time you shrink to fit one, a little of your spirit suffocates.

What Happens When You Burn the Box

When you stop trying to fit the mold, everything changes:
- You start speaking without filtering for approval
- You stop waiting for permission to lead
- You let your difference become your distinction
- You stop chasing acceptance and start building alignment

You realize that the only thing you ever needed was *yourself,* fully expressed and unapologetically alive.

Action Challenge: Burn the Box (Symbolically)

Make a list of every role, label, or identity that has tried to define you:
- Too loud
- Too sensitive
- Too driven
- Not feminine enough
- Not "enough" for a man, a church, a career, a culture

Write them out on paper.

Then — tear it up. Burn it. Throw it away.

Now replace it with a new declaration. Write it in bold, post it where you can see it:

"I am not here to fit in. I am here to stand out."

ROOT WORK

1. Box Audit
Ask yourself:
- Where in my life am I still performing to be accepted?
- What silent rules am I obeying that no longer serve me?
- Who benefits when I stay boxed — and why have I continued to comply?

Now pick one box — and begin exiting it.

2. Journal Prompt
"What would my life look like if I stopped trying to be acceptable and started living authentically?"

Visualize it.
Write it out like it's already yours.
What would you wear? Say? Build? Decline?

Then commit to one action this week that aligns with that vision.

3. Daily Declaration
"I am not too much. I am perfectly designed for my calling.
I will no longer shrink for comfort or compromise for approval."

Truth to Hold On To

They told you to stay in your lane. But you were never meant to drive their road.
You were born to design your own route — and ignite the pavement as you go.

PART IV:

Influence & Impact — Owning Your Presence

This time, you're not starting from scratch. You're starting from strength.

— For Every Woman Who's Starting Over —

Chapter 19:

The Single Season

... Chapter 19: The Single Season

It's not the waiting room. It's the training ground.

This chapter is for the women the world tries to pity.
The women they label as "cat ladies," "too picky," "hard to love," or "intimidating."
This is for the woman who chooses *not* to settle — and is misunderstood for it.

The truth is, singleness is not a punishment. It is a divine positioning.

It's not a space to be ashamed of — it's sacred. It's where the deepest parts of you are rebuilt, redefined, and reawakened.

What the World Says vs. What Strategic Grace Knows

Society whispers:
- You're running out of time
- You're only valuable if someone else chooses you
- If you're still single, you must be doing something wrong

Strategic Grace says:
- You're being prepared, not punished
- This is your season of intentional alignment
- You are choosing *wisely,* not desperately

The single season isn't where life pauses.
It's where you begin living on purpose — without compromise.

Why Singleness Is Strategic

In singleness, you are unfiltered.
No mirrors. No distractions. Just you — and God.
You hear yourself clearly.
You discover what excites your spirit, what disturbs your peace, and what you truly deserve.

This is the season where:
- Your schedule belongs to you
- Your dreams are pursued without detour
- Your healing is prioritized without interference
- Your growth isn't negotiated to appease someone else's ego

You're not "waiting."
You're building.
You're blooming.
You're becoming.

And the love that will meet you on the other side of that?
It won't *complete* you.
It will *complement* the masterpiece you've already become.

Action Challenge: Court Yourself

This week, take yourself on a date.
Not just a casual night in — an intentional experience of celebration and love.

- Get dressed like you're meeting your soulmate
- Take yourself to dinner, the museum, a concert — whatever lights you up
- Write yourself a note of gratitude
- Speak to your reflection with kindness and honor

Then ask:

"What have I been waiting to receive from someone else — that I now choose to give myself?"

Now give it. Fully. Unapologetically. Joyfully.

ROOT WORK

1. The Joy List
Make a list of ten things you *genuinely* love doing alone.
Not because you're settling — but because they energize and affirm you.

Examples might include:

- Morning walks
- Cooking for yourself
- Reading by candlelight
- Weekend getaways
- Creating something with your hands

Commit to doing at least one item from that list every week this month. You are worth investing in.

2. Journal Prompt
Ask yourself:

"Where am I still waiting for someone else to choose me — instead of choosing myself first?"

Write freely. Be honest.
Then ask: "What version of me is waiting on the other side of this choice?"

3. Daily Declaration
"I am not in limbo. I am in preparation.
This is not a delay — it's divine development.
I am not half of anything. I am whole."

Truth to Hold On To

This season isn't about lack. It's about becoming the woman who will never again be lost in someone else.
Because she finally found everything she needed — in herself.

Influence & Impact — Owning Your Presence

A partner doesn't complete you.
The right one multiplies you.

— Marriage, Grace, and Mission —

Chapter 20:

Marriage, Grace, and Mission

... Chapter 20: Marriage, Grace, and Mission

A partner doesn't complete you. The right one multiplies you.

We've been told a story — a fairytale, really.
That the prize at the end of womanhood is a partner. A wedding. A ring.
That once you say "I do," you've arrived.
But what if marriage isn't the destination — it's the divine assignment?

Too many women reach the altar not to commit, but to surrender.
Not just to the person they're marrying — but to an outdated belief that their purpose now takes second place.

They trade:
- Clarity for compromise
- Voice for validation
- Calling for compatibility

But marriage, in the context of Strategic Grace, is not about erasing yourself.
It's about evolving — with someone who honors your full expression.

What Marriage Looks Like in Strategic Grace

Marriage isn't just romance — it's stewardship.
It's not the soft music and vows alone. It's the daily decision to protect each other's peace, power, and purpose.

Marriage built on grace means:
- **You collaborate for legacy, not compete for control**
- **You protect each other's dreams instead of pressuring them into silence**
- **You nurture faith, emotional safety, and growth**

True partnership doesn't ask you to *dim* to fit — it invites you to *expand* to thrive.

If you feel you must mute your calling to "keep the peace," it's not peace. It's pretense. Pretense means you're faking it. Whether for family, appearances or social media. It's still fake and built on quicksand and eventually you will sink.
And it's a red flag wrapped in tradition.

Mission Over Just Emotion

Love should feel good.
But it should also *build* something.

A mission-driven relationship doesn't only stir your heart — it strengthens your purpose.
It should activate your next level.
It should birth something beyond you both.

Ask yourself:
- Are we growing spiritually, mentally, and emotionally?
- Do we sharpen each other — or just soothe each other?
- Do we have a vision for where this is going that goes beyond convenience and chemistry?

The mission isn't just to fall in love.

It's to build legacy, move in purpose, and stand in power — together.

Action Challenge: Write Your Relationship Mission Statement

Whether you're married, dating, healing, or preparing — define your vision for partnership.

Write a Relationship Mission Statement using prompts like:
- "In this relationship, we commit to…"
- "Together, we will…"
- "Our relationship will be a space where…"

Let this statement guide your expectations, decisions, and boundaries. Use it as your compass, not just for love — but for alignment.

ROOT WORK

1. Alignment Inventory

If you're currently partnered:
- Where are you flourishing together?
- Where are you silently sacrificing?
- Where are you deeply aligned — and where do you need realignment?

If you're currently single:
- What will you no longer compromise on in love?
- What patterns or red flags will you no longer ignore?
- What kind of support and purpose-driven partnership are you preparing to receive?

2. Journal Prompt
"What kind of love do I believe I deserve — and who taught me that?"

Was it modeled by your parents? Defined by your past? Shaped by trauma?

Now rewrite the narrative.

What kind of love *will you* believe in from this moment forward — and why is it rooted in your worth?

3. Declaration
"I will never again lose myself to be loved.
The love I give — and receive — will never come at the cost of my voice or vision.
My marriage, whether now or in the future, will multiply my mission — not muffle it."

Truth to Hold On To

The best relationships aren't built on perfect people — they're built on mutual protection of purpose.
Marriage isn't about completing each other.
It's about becoming more whole — together.

✨ Final Words

This is the work.
Not the performance. Not the pretend peace.
But the root-deep, power-filled, grace-soaked becoming of the woman you were always meant to be.

You were made for more.
Not louder. Not faster. Not prettier.

More *you*.
More presence.
More legacy.

And that begins, and ends, with **Strategic Grace**.

And remember this: God made the ceiling out of glass for two reasons.

1. So you can *see through it.*
To remind you that the goal isn't invisible — it's *within reach.*
He gave you vision to keep climbing.

2. So you can *shatter it.*
Because what was once meant to contain you will now be proof of how far you've risen.

Don't just tap the glass.
Break it — boldly, loudly, unapologetically.
Walk through it, and don't look back.

"For we are God's masterpiece.
He has created us anew in Christ Jesus,
so we can do the good things He planned for us long ago."
— Ephesians 2:10 (NLT)

You are His masterpiece.
You are the work — and the worker.
The vision — and the vessel.
The force — and the grace.

So keep rising.
Keep glowing.
Keep becoming.

Burn every box.
Break every ceiling.
And build what they said you never could.

Because your life is the evidence.
And your next level begins — and ends — with **Strategic Grace.**

www.ingramcontent.com/pod-product-compliance
Lightning Source LLC
Chambersburg PA
CBHW071013120626
46546CB00003B/1067